THE CHARGES

Other books by Albert Cook

THE DARK VOYAGE AND THE GOLDEN MEAN
THE MEANING OF FICTION
OEDIPUS REX: A MIRROR FOR GREEK DRAMA
PROGRESSIONS (poems)
THE ODYSSEY (verse translation)
THE CLASSIC LINE: A STUDY IN EPIC POETRY
PRISMS: STUDIES IN MODERN LITERATURE
THE ROOT OF THE THING:
THE BOOK OF JOB AND THE SONG OF SONGS
ENACTMENT: GREEK TRAGEDY
MIDWAY (poems)

THE CHARGES

ALBERT COOK

THE SWALLOW PRESS INC.

CHICAGO

Published by
The Swallow Press Incorporated
1139 S. Wabash Avenue
Chicago, Illinois, 60605

LIBRARY OF CONGRESS CATALOG CARD NUMBER 70-112872

Acknowledgements

Arts and Literature, The Circle Review, Jeopardy, Massachusetts Review, Niagara Frontier Review, Poetry: a Magazine of Verse, Quixote.

Again for Carol

CONTENTS

I

II

IV

I

Again and Again

Wie soll ich meine Seele halten, dass
Sie nicht an deine rührt

In the valley shadows this fire is a ghost, love,
If rain quivers the air. The white sheet
Of rain will not overcome an illumined house
Owed, whether won or lost, the first time.
Where is the shadow of green
I know for an illumined garden?
If lost in the fire, where is the reason for being?
My ghostly sister's hair glistens in one or the other.
Her thigh shudders, and we are side by side.

Airy fire gives the rain a reason for being
In the lost stakes of the green garden, if so.
My love is the sister I miss in another garden
I know. My illumined sister, under the weight of the house,
You shudder, lost, before the fire.
A second fire owes its illumination
Not to the rain.
If by the mountainous shadows I know where we are,
Who am I to have won?

The fire well lost is illumined a second time.
The house ill won gathers mould.
The love, my love, never won, is never lost
A second time, no fire. Love carries its debts on its head
Like a mountain wife carrying water
Into illumined air won again and again.
I and my reason for being live side by side
In debt and rain and love. If the mountain moves,
It is known.

Where the Wanderers Fold Their Tents

Where the wanderers fold their tents
In the yellow desert of mercy and numberless sands,
I am bred to be numbered down to the grains
Of age in my hair.
I am not brought around to the absolute blue
Of the blind sea, the hill
Buries its dream of bell buoys under bells.

The all-eyed Book is numbered with the fields
Of goldenrod. Pollen ascends
On its own. Sojourners, bred to come around,
You pitch your ordered tents at the heart
Of my expectation.
Number is as number does.
My merciless age surrounds none other than me.

Sad-eyed friends, do not bury the yellow floors
As though the blue sky folded mercies. They are there
Without number or the staggering eyes of bells.
To number the tents are blind.
I am bred to mercy in the yellow-eyed wings
Of bell-risen butterflies.
Ox-headed suppliants charge with their eyes.

Would they number mercies they might violate?
The fields of one-eyed wheat
Scatter them in a deadening sand.
The mercy-laden head is Argus-eyed.
Inch by inch the ageless column rounds ahead.
When the yellow drifts are gone,
The inbred grains are stored on a straight-eyed hill.

Let Your Friend Descend
From His Apartment at Twilight And

(The tests, the retorts, the inundations
Fathered forth upon an inscrutable heir
Who worries and wonders, not
Subject to wonder——

Whose hands, were he the person he had always hoped
To be, with too much delight on his hands for idleness,
Would overflow like a sturgeon
Fisherman's in a good year——)

Follow his body and shadow-spirit down an elevator
And out to your accompaniment. The minute
You posit pride
Of his simple pride,

Pride on pride, the storeyed houses come tumbling down
In the eye; which are visibly standing. So that won't do,
Whatever it tells
Of his divination

When on his knees or in the shining, revelatory dark.
Call your shots, which are his. Pretend you could hear the penny drop,
Plums ripen, women weep, men
Thunder with silent fists.

Start from the tongue you have in common, or invite him
To unbend. He will go on in the rarity of open air
To be taken in by shrubs
And porcelain skies

And by the high-strung wires and rocky outcroppings
You are perched among willy-nilly. He has pushed through leaves

Of branches and come out,
A bulky revenant,

Not allowing the placid metamorphoses
Of district ponds to influence his whereabouts,
Tagging along.
The sagging boles

Of less than enough pleasurable groves
Give way. There are not enough old friends within earshot
Keen to interpret
Speaking silences

Somewhat the way metronomic tongs measure pleasurably
By aftertwang. The apocalyptic stars fall
Where they may, and both of you
Stay undismayed.

He is left, consequently, with a burden of saying
That the red seepages of an unabashedly admired
Sunset on his hands
Are as good as demotic blood,

De la Tour's translucent blood, Lawrence's voices
Of its devices. There are enough voices falling
From the air's ragbag
To create their havoc.

The gas flame above the factory burns away
Below the flashing signs and airplane-throbbing dark.
The topmost remainder
Of fall leaves burns away.

Let be. Let him be, his back turned to your meant
Friendliness. It comes back to his being the one
Who would never
Have forgiven himself

Were it not for the mitigating circumstances
Of life all loose ends and live wires, to invent
What cries for lack
Of needing invention.

The Child Who Has Vanished, Abides

His mirror no longer reveals
The child that the willow
Takes in as a matter of course and the streams
Gaily pass by. The bodily organs
All outdo themselves to please him in their concert.
And he listens.
The echoes go farther and farther.
To listen is never in vain.
The mountains shake the trees he had never seen.
And the mirror brightens no less to take in the ruddy
Bursts of gunfire he did not
Register, first time around. To freeze into silence
The open mouths of orating senators.
Against those actual noises, the mirror reveals
A face that has aged,
And the keening
Of the undimmed child stays still as the quicksilver
Face on which he seems
Falsely to have wholly died.
He has never been more alive.

Driven Through Death

Mourners, you cannot
come to terms with the beyond
               it is terror numbs
               the whole life of its triumph
               grief strives to reconcile
and pay attention, wrapped up
in your escorted procession of shiny cars
flying small flags of identification
around the stripped park,
warmed but by hope of a new day where a
stripped park, stiff by its nature, would pay
no attention either.

Terror numbs and hope consoles,
so long as sight blesses
Eyes conceiving second sight, making
First sight what it has always been:
triumphant, terrorized.

This fire of grief cannot make it come clear.
The void of a death deprives your senseless world
of senses you were tricking. The triumph and wholeness
of a soul's death when whole releases terror.
He may have been complete: his completeness
Is your incompleteness,
His triumph your terror, once the consolation
for him cannot be one for you.
               When scarce the just shall be secure
               Terror makes not the living pure,
               Triumph for them cannot endure,
               That, if it was attained,
               Must for the dead.

And the paradisal

9

joys stay ungrasped (except as anticipated)
       by definition
               And tears
Have power, power
they are the first to mourn.
After the stone
           had been pushed away
when he had called into the dark of the cave and Lazarus
Came forth

Jesus! Wept!

To transcend death does not wipe away death's tears
makes no clean sweep.
The strong-breathed mourners live beyond their tears
putting great stock
              in memories of many brotherhoods.
The drawer of glass shuts darkness on the key
     to nothing.
            And you are back
in the odorless houses buffered so that terror
cannot shake them or triumph sweep them up,
houses that outlast their terrible, triumphant inhabitants
to the naked eye alone.

East o' the Sun, West o' the Moon

I walked by the common river
A half a life ago
Down from the lofty city
To wonder what I knew.

No clue lay in the children's eyes
Rising to the sun,
Lulled like mine as the simple clock
Stood darker in the moon.

Released from picture classes
We bounded to our play,
Never too close to the looming house,
Never too far away.

And spoke but seldom listened,
Checked but seldom thought
Save in the lone marrow
That nothing might be taught.

Sun and moon in the head began
Their pulse, insisting as
The pearl's grain rounds in a shell
Where pain nor glimmer was.

And I said to my absent mother,
"When do the sun and the moon
Dwindle and no more matter
Than a house key?" Even then,

Never, I knew, was the answer,
Though nothing else I knew.
Distance stood as still as time.
Our auto flew and flew.

I dreamt my smiling father
Had nothing to replace
But I would swindle my poor self
To say it to his face.

In the stillness of no answer
My wonder daily grew.
White lines sank in the playing field.
The suffering lived alone.

Houses rocked and cars unleashed
What could not be talked away.
Each bye-and-bye mother's lintel
Throbbed in our wavering eye.

The river was thick, sun and moon
All as far as an eye could see
Disenchanted no waker
From stirred perplexity.

Perplexed like a kinless person
Lost in so much ado
To find or name what would be his home,
I slackened through and through.

Hand fell short like a setting sun
Of many a silent plea,
While the new grown, sure and calm
Got this and that in fee.

And all about minds made it up
That this would never do
And cut the garment to the cloth
And moved glib and unfree

To wear the latest collar
And keep the season young
Or stand on a deck rapt to hear
The ship's shattering horn;

To buy and sell, say and unsay,
To shrink to understand,
To love a mirror's fullness or
A pillar in the sand.

The river calmed, sun and moon
Kept my own regular hours.
My voice, for the time never failing,
Had fully learned its powers.

The key that sparks my motor
So long as it holds fast
Hangs on the same ring as the key
That opens up my house.

Yet wonder is driven deeper
And everyone but seems.
Out in open farm country
Of white collar dreams

Bushes are staled by animals,
A long fence strained by snow.
What it is still chiefly palls
Wisps and I fail to know.

At the broad source of the river
Lost in the dens and din
Of a city set as on a cliff
I drew my nurture in

As lungs draw in the terrible
Gasps of mountain air
Above where anything can grow.
None the descent will dare.

While kingdom and King of heaven
Beyond sun and moon do lie,
His Mother's bosom sorrows are
Outbrandishing the sea.

The sun goes down in dragon's blood,
The moon swells like a sigh,
And on the verge of every night
I swallow a bigger why.

Impulsions

The mouth of a lonesome father pushing the underbrush
Open for his passage gapes alive under a drooping moustache.

The clean-shaven director pulls his cigar out of his mouth
To shout "Come on out!" and the reel freezes in the glare.

I know that the sometime dumb cry out, that the craven, riven
By hidden harmonies, moult their fears. The photographer clicks
A heartbreak wordlessness, strong enough to hold the shot.

I have been walking under
Elms all my life.

Willed aftermath of wonder,
Wild foretaste of decay.
Blunders persist
And turn the heart to clay.

And others seek robust salvation in the confrontation of blood,
Damned by the conflagration of all they hold dear.

The stone budges free. Once inside the rugged mouth of the cave,
A cavern smell weakens its hold on the air, the dark soil
Holds its moisture, musty rocks roughen exploring hands.
Out in air an age later the packed lunch to the ravenous
Is sweet.

Small of the year,
Smell of the sea.

Sketches of darkness bloat themselves on my kind elation,
Spunk peters out. Swatches of darkness are organizing
My blue funk.

As though kings could toast the sea in goblets more flashing
Than the insurge of waves over and over, by holding them high!

Amorists alive in the glare of spaced lemon trees
Plunge into sheer water, prelude to a softer plunge
Into each other's whitenesses, protected from that sun
Streaming off their navels, a foam born love may turn a burning
Coal, lover lover comes poignantly the dying cry
Easing themselves into the black tangle of matrimony
To domesticate all the terrors blinking
With as many eyes from coverts as multiplying fears.

Thin surrogates are played out, thick meadows extravagantly
Dapple daisies, stars of foam on a sea of waving straw.
The dairy farmer shoulders his overalls, dew thickens his grass.
The dairy herds will be browsing in the mash of grass, machines
Gleam glumly in the barn standing as ever on his hill,
Bourne, byre, pasture, while the one-time boy seasons
Into old age until his own grown boy take or a neighbor buy
The whole show to truck the cans of sweet milk round the roads.

I yearn asunder
Country gloom
Unlearn the game
Of sitting tight.

Schooled daughters of despondency clap their hands for the music's
Discordancies, serving for the festive midnight strong drink.
The violist is nowhere for this chilly pause
On his narrowing circuit and the fuzzy laws
He has long forgotten how he learned to tolerate.

Had I been brought to the quick of steely circumstance
I would have tempered my unruly sympathies
In the absolute gentleness of the equanimous.

The flow of papers across a backbreaking desk
Drains the head's vestiges of spontaneity.

The overjoyed mother abounds, saddening abundance
Into overripening, her mere sweetness will call the tune
For nothing more than being on her own inundated
By the minor concerns of a slack debilitation.

The repair man tinkers with one machine till it runs
And then another. The fine student rides high changing
Schools. The playing field absorbs the élan of youth.
The self-regulating shutters of the skyscraper do not calm
The secretary inside who keeps checking her mirror's slate
In effective readiness.

She takes down
The etching words, he turns away through the open window
Into the decline of his life, the gradual slope
Prepared for in the cushions of actuarial foresight.

The strictly taught scion of abstemious parents is
Lean for the clankings of a newly programmed era. The future
Does not draw huzzahs, and the past deepens in a dark fold.

Myth moth mouth
Priming the likeness of a skeleton swaying
The charmed flesh shrouding
It and every other.
The open-omened driver levitating along
The freeway will be trading his soft pedal and nervous wheel
For the converse of the suited men he has worn down
To dynamic mutuality, white shirt and sombre tie.

I am adrift in flimflam.

A glazed Buddha
Presides over an
Alcove of ferns.

Palled and barred, parried and still bold
I adjust my hold calmly.

The king size bed
Lulls as it unlimbers
The bathed
Couple.

The tense husband
Does not return
Till after midnight
From the microscopically
Infected jelly
Refrigerated
In his lab.

I will not
Belie making
The bed and being
Swallowed until
I emerge
Alive
Thereupon,
Of the cleansed
Energies
Hostage and
Celebrant.

Dwellers and the Dweller

The vanishing of loveliness is such,
The hands fold open that had laid it out.
The reader sees no weeds. The hunter
Comes out into a clearing, his boots
Caking on the sole, heavier and clumsier,
As though he had abandoned reason and slept
In a cave of his own making, bearded man
Of the Golden Legend, walking abroad.

The old child, doer, the new actor
Rises, rises and knows what he had come for.
Theatre gives way
To city, altar to city, and the tombs
Are banished to the woods. Another day
Turns its transparent page.
A heartbroken girl
Settles for less than marriage. A man rebuffed
More than once, stops fighting back. He never will get through.
The ring gets tighter and its edges break.
Wrong gets no righter in the labyrinth
Of advocacies.
The marble step lets the glass vault bare itself.
Never will the money filter tame
Through chosen or choosing hands.

The rulers in the grip of their desires
Turn on their pedestals, struggle so they may
Stay invisible to shouting crowds.
The blank faced sufferer turns on his heel.
Hunger that is too wide to know
Comes from behind, the touch
Of someone loved too far
Away to see makes its appearance known.

The Barriers You Erect with Words

The barriers you erect with words
Designed to melt them are your quandary.
Days are swallowed down their well.
She has kept a certain distance. Somehow
The open door brings you closer, the clean bed
Repulses close up where you had hoped to thrash it out.
Desk, car, uniform, so many leaves
Falling from a naked branch
Where a ruffled bird issues from his beak his tape
Encapsuling the possibility
Of delighting an ear not so designed.
The car stops short at the well's
Well-coigned rim of stone, the man
In the uniform marries a vast indifference.
The barriers are visible if built
By invisible hands and orders
Are a way of acting. Give a desk its due
If it gives nothing to you.
The clean bed swallows its distances.
Wind thrashes the leaves.
The ruffled bird takes wing at a simple word.

Music, music!

Ah for the time I am one, enraptured hearing
Chords
Stars in the heaven where I was to go
As though already there and filled with love
Eros it is clear breasts this labyrinth
Of sound like all the others tremblingly bearing
Love

             And all about
Fountains and the fountain's
Bell answers this sigh clearly the great plain
Bears overabundance of grain the great
City grinds in arrogated power

Kyries of mothers resound in the gold
Vaults of chapels, humble heads not craned

Fire roars easily where rakers are
Heaping high for fires the gold eyed leaves
They shall not see again
Is this all a holy wilderness
To be heard over the pitiable nothing-
Rinsing and money-milked air waves
The twittering machines
Go on about their rounds

             It is I I
Who rise for the major proclamation
Dinned
In my ears dinning I who am to die
A time unknown as music's intervals
Charge on ahead, time full as music done

And I break in

21

Fatal dialogue
I am trundled on the vanishing trains
Jostled boomed blamed unblamed
I impose on the imposing
Darkness that pacifies my itching ears
And long to swim where there might
Spas be powdering the sandy verge
Porch lights switch lights search lights Japanese lantern
Lights headlights
I spend myself
Remember
Turned upside down a musical
Theme or plaything of a snowstorm under a bell of glass
On a black pedestal
Music of Christmas and I am constrained
Like a prisoner at Christmas forgive me prisoners

I ground out my time it flashed diamond
Grinding
I burbled in an imaginary revival
Floating bloated along the damned stream
I unnaturally
Blasted the natural face and its precious form
Rapt
Love is a loadstone
Space takes up all the forms the Pump Room
The Ovens the Potter's Field the Palm
Island *Aigues Mortes*
I crusade as though to heaven

I crusade as though the king
From *Aigues Mortes*
Welcoming the caroling

Holy wilderness
Made not to unmake unfailingly
To bless and not be unblest, hear singing sung
Upheavals fade out like denials
Da capo
Have broken with the drudging and am whole
In this imagination blunt
Instrument no longer blunt by dint of being ground

Strung lights and *aves* sung
Dispel no loneliness for the original
Dispellers of loneliness wife mother
And sisters the stitch in Adam's
Rapt side forever

                Muster a mastery
I destroy I did try and tried will
Trapped straining
Stroked like a gut string
Wondering and rewondering
A phosphorescence of decay a health
Threatening to fail and failing

Possibilities miring possibility

And still I quicken to the glorious discovery
Not to possess the deadening power
Of hardening the heart an ear of stone
The musical earth is filled with stone
                          Heaven
And earth are full of Thy glory.

Mystery

1.

Mystery
        the impenetrable mystery
Does not change
           all else is changeable

By which (its standing still) it is known to be
The mystery we pass through, the lives,
Mechanisms, rites of passage, modes
Of accomodation, all the desperate
Gestures of hope toward
Salvation in mystery.
           Two men
Are met in its name
           A man and a woman
A host
           Met in its name
Leaves wilt
        Bottles empty
               Hearts give out
The name changes, it changes not
Since the beginning of time, a beginning it straddles
As we are found to be essaying, like as not
Succeeding (a mystery).

2.

        The grey
Buildings have not moved, I have moved.
           They are cleaned.
I come clean among them, if it were possible,

Mimicry in the full bloom of time
Of redemption there is no diverging from.
                        The river
Moves past the trees-weight of green leaves below.
The cathedral wall.
                        It had not moved.
        Promenade of my dallying
                        You have not moved.
Aging is simply aging after all,
No mystery
                mystery lies
Elsewhere, through this screen
Of separations poignantly to be discerned
From unions never quite realized.

Through You

Through you
ritual of languor
superbness
ritual of splendor
through you
nipple membrane enclosure
flesh walls, flesh vistas
gargoyled, adjustable, not given
to excesses of restraint
(bound faun: a nagging
impossibility)
silent concerts
round tables
                    dream
shared like the real one is
hungrier far than the other.

Faun in the reeds,
nights of fishing,
through you
Swiss nights, delicious chills, mountain lake,
brass band
rituals of exploring retrogression
expansion advancement
through you, never mind
squarely in the beachcombed
middle
through you
harpsichord plucking
heartstrings
through you
rituals of flesh through heartstring
rituals

through you
realization
suburban
audible
music
through you
sympathy
thick tongued oracles
imaginary
coracles bent of trees that drank light
supple in you
poem without verb
through you.

2.

Verb I make or mar, our naked grace
Governs a visible harmony and trains
Unwilling tendrils, let it be, let be.

We are not bothered if we run the race
Or never when a carping friend refrains,
Highlighting boldly our fragility.

We comb our share of joy and hail the trace,
Welcoming air whether it shines or rains
Around the motions loud with you and me.

3.

I recapitulate
through you

I don't mind vegetating
when you do
I ape
Your yielding
and it sits well on me
through you
I digress without
losing my center
It is heartening
through you.

I am polyglot, a
stone idol,
oblivious of being an embittered backslider,
I feel my fault weather away, wither away
Through you.

Otherwise

I am supposed to have the tact, supposing
I have the power, not to speak of the fate
Surrounding me, charged
With myself.

                       My boldness, my indifference,
Unburdening solitariness.
                 Pardon me.
But the Chinese moon in a mountain lake
Will sing like the trout breaking its surface
Without a vocalic sound, still splash or plash.

Why otherwise was the inverted boor
Of a northern king
Castled in *Sans Souci?*
And she, most rich when she could stand being utterly
Poor, knew
And wrote down, out of obedience,
The interior
Castle of vision, pearl of the grain of sand
Which is the world we know.

Dreamt dreams becloud the scanning eyes.
Their fluency escapes.
Through us
The Will darts unerringly
Like an airplane on its beams.
                    Exhaust zooms
Inundate our machicolations.
So let the several griefs
               Couple and die
               Their fluency escapes as does exhaust.

And have their part.

As may lindens by the lake

Moons and trout

castles by the sea

Above the stinking flats.

Otherwise I would be
Dumb as the Greeks called fish
Without a ripple:
A goat
Eating the label off a tin can under the unheeded
Zoom of an airplane.
Bah!

Otherwise . . . but it all
Lives in and with us,
All the way to the polycephalic Hindu gods
And hierarchies,

to the serene

Hellenic manifestations of godlike power,
As the dark feelings do
That brought them out of darkness into light,
Ex nihilo.

Snow-blowing Winds Are no More to Be Believed

Snow-blowing winds are no more to be believed
For all their wildness than the humming ones.
I am humoring
The dunce I have always been.
Why do we never listen
To the inner cry?

The whole harming
Show will have passed through the door of my eyes
Like a harrowing wind, and I none the wiser.
You are left inside as a humming heart
Wondering if I have really passed up
What we always lost,

And in our good time
May well have won, though the soon-stopped mouth
In its homing, would not have found it out.
The full moon holds out windlessly.
It and we come whetted out
On the other side.

Transparencies

Exchanging greetings I go on my daily round
As if my sun-burnished forehead
Were impenetrable. You teach me it is not.
Daily, gaily, you troop through it. I am a decal
Of you, your transparency.
Your sorrows are my sorrows. My dreams
Founder where they may but are buoyed up
In your wash of reclamations through me.
And it does me good. So St. Augustine
Dried the eyes that wept for Dido dead.
Transparent, yes, I dread the stream
Of penetrations. How otherwise?
I fashion a blank I for lances to break on
And they shiver right on through, naturally.
How otherwise? The law is engraved
On the glass of my being.
My mirror dims and never disappears.
Lord, I would have swindled my very self
In the vain attempt to swindle you.
This way I am moved and not given
To a deadening of activity.
Clear as glass. This way the dream of slowing
Down harms no one. A struck match flares
In my all-encompassing gloom. This way
The trodden chicken and the sleepy mule
Tread my earth. This way no man opaque
Is herded to his desert.
Singing wires and singeing fires
Plunge on
As dolphins encircle a coin or hounds a stag
On tapestry bounded in needlework
Of galleries I could not have foreknown
And dare see. Ships draw near my shoals.

In my disarray trees sway the other way
Unimposing. I cannot help absorbing
As a stream absorbs. Let me not be
The hero whose absorptions honeycomb
An existence buzzing with sweets for everyone
And the one in the center dies
Like everyone, having seen through the arts of life
And been seen through.

II

The Charges

Forget not for long the long eye-opening
Crest and savor of a morning's love, I had borne
My forgetting who could barely remember
What I left
Behind me streaming, and none
Had been named, planted in space
Or been plucked up.

In the small hours the ponderous street-cleaning machine forces the
      charge
Of its jet, and the circular brushes, along the dead leaves
And trash of the asphalt, I turn over and listen, I know
Where I am

Antennae are out and bend back
The announcer keeps streams of data
Flowing through his voice
And will never divorce.

Peonies are eaten open by ants
Pears are ripening
Ladders crashing through fire
A bride and groom ever too young
Name on the tongue
Life on the line
Mine is
I begin again
Imitatio Christi

Carry on gentleness in the charge of force,
Deadly neutrality, divine
Equanimity

The blind god comes on me widening and lightening
There is no place for other gathering and praise
There is every place
He is bound and freed
Quia amore langueo, and languishing
Defeats itself.

And when the avocado seed swells, something
Splits it clean to grow.

Apples pressed for cider
Fertilize the ground, musty smell
On the frosty air,
I stand under the airlanes, someone
Is flying over the spongy crowns of trees.

Each time it's all there.

Do not let the face of what I am telling myself I am
Get lost, the old friend
Got crocked to forget the rage of the squabble
He sobered up and sweated into,
Going through the motions of swimming and diving
Fucking and dreaming will not do
Jump through the hoop
Of no war but the rare just war.

The man who claimed to be dieted
On mere complacency did so on fraud.

Fret into being, worry out of a quandary
In ten years that friend was a drunkard
The charge of a habit

Does not violate
Its laws of increase.

A chalked face is scrawled on a placard,
The panchromed endorser of Canadian Club rides Bahaman sharks.
The government lawyer chokes back
Rage against frittering and lets his senses
Dwindle.

Hitler has won, we are charged with his *Gesamtkunstkrieg.*
Strangle on that, the man so powerful
He can forget his lies, short-circuited
In his very power, when all is said and done.

They have begun with the golden
Number of proportions in a man
And end with the model of a brain, matter
And threads devised by a brain, dustless under celluloid.
Put a large section of the brain to sleep
Cut it away
Shock it dead
Desperation.

Need deforms a man blinded by need.

To his apartment
Gaudily fitted out within
The white-haired singer in *The Student Prince* retreats, sodden
And hypocritical, homosexual
And Puritan, diamond-stickpinned, weeps into a mirror wrought
With wooden roses, detached
From his mother's vanity.

Open the half-world
Of erotic self-glorification, self-
Rending, there is no way
To ground the glory of the gift of you
Short of an infinite
Reach to the other, stepping free
Of a nightgown, candid flank,
Blue beating at the soft inside of her elbow,
Soft breast and its swollen nipple, hip
Curving to the hirsute center, yours if hers,
Faithful to the Gordian toils, ends
You were devised for,
pur lepton, subtle fire,
If you have come through, stepping free
Into a clear source
Charging bestowals.

The pale glowworm is indolent over night-misty leaves.

I presume to turn
My whole being to this self-
Gratification, I am called,
Back, the charge of multitudinous voices,
My salvation.

The several lives
I lead to hold together are pulling me apart.

Sancta simplicitas!

And if this blur
My outline, what if I do flex
Age-old idolatries, riding over

Out of the state of the hook-curved
Jelly-dibbled foetus of the color plate
Into the transfixing sway
Of pleasure, the plain orgasmic light.

Calming a glitter, let the greater calm
Take over as long as it will, close dooms.
A black clock on a brass-wrought pedestal
Dingles and drowns hours in a trembling gloom
Of so broad a room.

If this exhilaration be a long time dying
And I be squared, no charge
Of shame will overwhelm the overwhelming
Rise in me, spendidly setting sun,
When I am likewise in a balance, less
Amazing in its way if the sun were charging
My very shoulder, instant
Conflagration,
Or I have swallowed the host of the sun.

It never comes through, comes true,
I am where my sense of being had hoped
My arms could be outstretched.

Every cry
Is wrung forcibly, a cry
To wring a heart hardened by a lifetime
Of schooling to be deaf
Fascinates and binds
In an oblivion not aspired to,
My own.

All things draw away,
Gravely the mute stirrings will not wait, ordeal
Nietzsche went through.
Turin turns its avenues straight to the mountains.
He flamed the pages in a Persian's guise, his blood,
And elated in ordeal signed
Himself The Crucified,
Charging a wheelchair thereafter,
Smothered crucifixions,
Hitler gave Mussolini the *Gesammelte*
Werke in leather and gold.

And the pale self-driving Jewish wife cannot bring herself to face tł
    charge
Time absolves;
At the corner of the managed apartment building she knew as a gi
The druggist obliged her mother with drugs or their equal,
Money did not bind the unholy pair,
The poor addict faded into pain and the father
Remarried in a matter of months.

The student from Baja California quits school and opens
A tacos stand nearby, hot evenings
Over a sizzling grill, money.

Awaiting a prescription of radium treatment
He gets bedsores, persistent annoyance
Charging a monstrous boredom, awaits the ball scores.

Whirlwind of inaction.

On the stoutly taken wine
Of lunch the family-counsellor priest

Bemoans the young divorcees' or equivalents'
No way out, casuistry bends
Its net to find a way and still the net
Sways in the wind, an awakened woman's desire,
And what will be the fate
Of the bright, stiff, mannish violinist
Outgrowing her violin at fifteen into ideas
Of young divorcées or the equivalent?

And the (silver) rose
Of 1910 is the androgyne
Cavalier of the Rose cutting his teeth
Penetrating the Marschallin
Cadenza
Of love in love with dying while her own
Man charges through brush after a boar
In the Bohemian forest
Figure of exquisite
Ridicule
Holding back, and the point is the fiancee
Of seventeen's equally dying love's
Sung paradise.

The floated petals are the breathing ones
I hail, the garden
Opens its endless day
When it closes over its own time under the angel's
Sword, charge,
Blade of glass warped straight across the gulf of a bed.
The fuller park is now, paradise,
Weltpunkt, Weltraum, Weltanschaung.

Misery's mystery dreaming a beginning,
In hoc signo vinces,
Charging the laps of mothers, heads of sons,
By this sign I live,
And it takes more,
The stiff elm leaf floats into morning
Light flanges, collops of light.

He who in the jaws of a night like no other
Is racked and gives up the ghost,
Knows the same.

Elation has overwhelmed him in his forty-ninth year,
He had never been a philosopher before,
And now has no need to be one.

Elms and the upblown leaves,
Roads and the great trunks, rooms and the straight eyes,
Hills and the path in a garden, every word
Uttered in love with me till my dying day, life
In eternity, who is to charge it
With being otherwise?

Evasions of Repose

If I forgot the hubbub and gave in
To a nagging for stagnancy . . This nonce . . .
My mossy ear was rankling like a sin
Hung in for fear of playing freedom's dunce,
And I am free to sag or rebegin.

The crow's wing dips a black, bedraggled tip,
Caw, caw! And the hawk indifferently
Plummets or soars over a gorge's lip.
My body is sharper in the eagle's eye
Than in my own, though I glimpse where to stop.

Where does it all leave me? Thought of repose
Does not unmist. Birds in fierce clarity
Repose when driven, that never can be wise.
My aspiration knows what it can be,
But haltingly. The wisdom comes and goes.

To One Whose Action Is of the Mind

For Don Coleman

A vision of green fields overreaching
Your stir of wishes like flourishing grass,
How could years' flaws be flensing and not bless
The adequacy that your unflinching sight
Rinses in doubling penance as in sleep,

Though your fierce grace is a far cry
From slumbers conceived of lulling till the moss
Thicken on stones shadows of lost joy,
And a river's still flow conduce alone
To the contentment of abandoning?

Such dreams persist with you so long as
The stress bright anonymity
Subjects you to has frozen its emphasis
Too deep, it might seem, for the caress of change,
Ice a foot thick, the river dark below.

There was a time you thought you had been given
Nothing the spirit does not opt for itself
And shadows of cloud grazed on an absent green.
River swelled aloof and broad. A stone
Brooded its weight, too somnolently grave.

Then it was you put off the helm of sleep
And let the dumb show, genially soft,
Of stone and green become you as it would
A river's rise or cloud's urged billowing.
Now if in afterthought you crave repose,

Think of that lost friend, a Sisyphus
Without the challenge of a hill, locked

In a ward outside whose window the lawn
Time's prissy strangulation keeps at bay.
He rolls the simulacrum of solid rock.

But you must bed in the long impress
Of what will come, or else the rock would
Collapse to a Madagascar cave flitting
With flibbertigibbet bats, or you pole at best
A pirogue through a bayou's Spanish moss.

Think your name at last may shine out so
Equal the river's, though some Pontine marsh
Wait a millennium to be drained,
And grass, grass bend to your concern,
More than genial softness coming to mind.

She Who Had Run the Gamut

She who had run the gamut of her joy
In self-absorption that expected more
Than she was left with, wishes her depths to stay
Unstirred, and lives in torment unless they are,
And lives her borne tepidities away.

Her afternoon glides like her driven car.
Blue mould softens on the orange she has not
Thrown away, and why do friends not appear
When you most need them? But to be forgot
May feed what being remembered could not bear.

The child unravelling her own desires,
The young girl craving and abhorring change,
The woman trailing the heavier floods of hers,
Languish as one. How could she not estrange
Plain gladness in the snail's pace of calm years

If operatic sentiments sponge
Up days, and wring them dry, and love, love
Creates no more enlightenment than ranges
Through paltry trusts she is despairing of?
The very window bears a melancholy tinge.

Ah not the tides of a fertile body's flood
Make the hands tremble burying her face,
But the astounding tenacity of a mood
Which aging drafters of Utopias
Would be dumbfounded to turn to any good.

The Deranging Preferences

Bells for the seasons
                tocsins have not gone out of style.
Not sighing, I prefer carilloning portals behind which
Destinies await my tending.
As though no one was ever known to be
The man of his preferences!
                As for those who sigh after *La Belle Epoque*—
If (it is) special out of all, then to a child.
The critical spirit is never known to the child.
Bells ride the four winds
In a cavity known to the mothers of the resigned.
                There are the ones who need
High winds
           Smoking proudly by a chosen fountain
   (some other epoch)
                The fountain dies in space
                Smoke is a trace of pride
                Pride—space of incredible hardnesses
                Where preferment takes place all the time.

The child, holding his breath in unbounded choosing, the spirit
Comes into its own.
The house shakes free of its owner's preferences.
The white rose, bred and planted, gone wild, floats
Free of its name.
                Freer of my name than of them,
I am the battler by day, the swimmer by twilight,
Swimmer of a summer's day,
Headwaters, backwaters,
Heard and heeded in a gloom of leaves.

There are the ones who make putty statues of ogresses;
           slack-jointed mannequins;

49

saw circus girls in half;
Who subject their other halves.
And to be idealized strains a girl taut
Preferring the strain of tautness wherein her preferences
        Are as it were deified.
                      The blonde Texas girl
Leans over to pry in the balloon-filled Indonesian restaurant
Behind the Pantheon, defending the South
    I have damned to the semi-refugee yellow proprietor-student of
                               International Law
Sitting, at my invitation, unimpressed, wearing
The (selfsame?) half-disengaged smile of the Chinese composer,
Recently widowed and so in the artist's colony,
Family incommunicado in the People's Republic,
Who drew out my Apologetics as I strung along
               In his Dauphine on the Thruway to New York,
    "If Christ saved the world,
        What about the Asiatic multitudes?"
Amid it all, sipping rose-petal wine from porcelain,
The blonde trades on her beauty like the black-panted,
Brown-eyed brown-velvet-filletted one
Ten years ago in the
California sun, choice
Of the burrowers into daylight
                   Lights in the head
Returning like slow bells.

It is enough to drive one to distraction
                off his head.
Their claims can never be amortized
           When they keep coming on.
           Wars
Killing to decrease the divergence

                    Widen the gap,
As the destructive spirit knows all along,
Driving itself to distraction.
All the constellated appurtenances of prayer
Do not stay them: with or without the brass name plate
        Pews follow hierarchies.
                    They like it that way. The chosen
Turn their dachas to face birches and flutterings
And the distracted are driven to Siberia
                Who once stood by the town gate
                    Singing or begging
Or wandered, prickly burrs, from town to town.
They have been gassed!
Have swooned, stoned.
They are tended and rarely mended
Or else unwound in the given hours of years
                Of tender attention, amortized
                    Questionably.
Our churchgoing forebears hid the deranged
                In the high head of a belfry
Whisking off in jangling coaches to the lives
                    That swarmed in the sorrowing
Head of the deranged.
                    The sacrifice took place
Late on a Sunday morning in a chapel clean
As the panes they had chosen not to stain,
As they were
As is.

Orison

Bare as a penitent
Whose joyed feet in the snow
Go numb and void, I show
My unencumbered bent.
The staggering Canossas
Have lured my soul away.

And I am none the less,
O luring cherubim.
Dreaming, I still may bless
Households of the proud
Dressed to kill and dim
Where the poor best are bowed.

The soldier I did not
Become, helmeted,
Ignores my dreamt headache and
Plunges his bayonet
In hard eyed aplomb
Through blood or through sand.

My easy cries are dumb.
Say I call deafness into play.
Abandoned to the will
Of an appalling dream,
I would give my playing body
Up to irising spray

And come out none the wiser
While nature thunders on.
Light lilts on spears of grass
While celebrations wane.
Out of his kingdom come
The heavy lover dies.

Twilit lilies bury
More than a weight of air,
Sunburst beyond the white
Beard of old Monet.
Before his war, our war.
I too will say my say,

Out of an inhuman
Pool, the skin wrinkling,
The mind played out
Or not induced to sing,
Heart of a better man
Shrivelling to a thing.

Divisions and disgrace,
Come martyrdom, come joy,
Nor taken are nor whelmed,
Thronging swallows and
Shimmery goldfish
Ingathered to one dream.

Hands for the Space of Wisdom

If the place you bought lay on an open wing
Your eyes would be shut, too wise.
I am stretching in wisdom and barely know what to do
With my fond hands.
The speed of the fish in the pond is likewise held up.
The surgeon braves his air.
You are fond of a new space, if anything.

Is it wise to gather speed if the fish in the space
Of the pond lies on the open wing
Of the water you bought and uses his eyes?
I have shut my hand, not knowing what to do.
The surgeon likewise opens his.
I place my fondness in stretching
The unbought time as it places the air of a face.

Your wise hands know they are not wings
If the place they hold up gives them the work of wings
To do or know how to do.
I am in the same place where the fond fish likewise
Is never still.
The wisdom of space braves our eyes.
The surgeon's eye is bought and knows what to bring.

Between Us

This soberness is longer than a night
Ending on rending, withersoever bound.
The rent got too high. You got through to me
At the airport. Smoking hard. Bitter thighs. Ties
To unrent ends. Unbending wills. A childhood's
Moods between us. Everyone. Angoraed breasts
Soften my anger. It comes up again.
Story of persons. Staring. Staring each other
Down, into a none-too-stranded night
Of embering and slumbering, of lashed
And captured cries. (I capture.) A wry face
Does not hamper proliferating lies
And losing. Making love again and again
Might have made us whole. Sugar in a bowl
Spilled one rainy morning between us.
Kleenex, *Job's Tears*, a near wall.
Eyes under shadow, shadowed mouth
Moistening the darkness between us, of light.
Blight brings hallucinogenic blight
To every component. A hangar loses us.
Globs. Sobs. We stall on steel stairs. A long map
Of our routes together unwinds in the vitals
Of one and the other. It spreads and spreads
Where you were and are. Opiates
For the flushed face weathered into its spate
Of trials into its further sobering cheer,
And jeers, tears, flights of fleering, fraught
With all it had computed, no less.
Jug-eyed sleepers massacre grief
And awake refreshed, sickening to recall.
The rain-cold horizon, bare of planes,
Opens a further one from its dewy self.

The Dimness of the Sea Scene

The swell
Of green slithers under blue
Like sheen on a mackerel,
Or darkens like the lunge
Of a hammer-headed shark.
                    Veil
Over my eyes, my eyes have pierced the veil
Of versions no longer bothersome.

> *And if a cloud of gnats*
> *Meets a heartfelt compliance?*
> *Limpidity*
> *Spells desire?*

And I have been stunned
By a birth of accords in a great calm.

Salt cakes on the rock.
After some days the white crust is visible,
Burled by snails, creatures pressed for the purple
Of the ancient world.

The bay, for a time, is a Circus Maximus,
Changeable, with strong influxes
Of drippling fog, of Persian
Crinklings of water, of alpenglow

> *And if what meets the eye,*
> *Iris over blue,*
> *ambiguous excellence,*
> *Evades revelation*
> *In the needle's eye, whose circumfere*
> *Is everywhere?*

The leaves of a bush take the light
As they find it, it finds them.
Seelenmusik, to face so dim a scene.

The fur-rubbing wings of a moth
Rub the night screen,

                    The fish's mouth
Is a tendon,

            The motions
I have made are not so assured.

Seeing is brandied fruit.

Seeing measures without
Variation or faltering
Or even undue haste
The felt pace heavenward.

Like a man glad though the motions he has made
Are not assured, the mountain rises out of mist.

To the Manner Born

My animal spirits take nourishment
From a cold and spirited day
And I am still all raw nerve,
To the manner born.

I am the gift I sold until too late,
I grub the leavings of an empty plate.
Never is it too late.
The windows as they are
Draw in a widowed green.
How could it go away?
I scrutinize a flaw.

And giving is a harder nut to crack
Than joy, which it empowers,
And the mind goes on reckoning its burdens
Evasively,
Not trapped in ungainliness but glorying
In the supposed need to ransack,
Become the meditation thought to be abhorred,
Harped on, heralded, dispraised.

One knobbly bone and a trembling star,
A ruined car, trawlers
Trawling, trawling, trawling in the sea.
I am the one who is burning
The candle of his life at both ends,
Reduced to volunteering.
I have not known the last impoverishment
When I sit upright reckoning
The self-imposed liabilities.

"Quit when you're ahead"
Has happened to the dead.
And all right I grant I could not be so moved without
Corresponding sacrifice, enabling
A man to say goodbye
To such hampered gestures, window, lawns,
Stars, moralizations, to the manner born.

If Idleness Were Strength, and So It Is

The cars outside my window
Glide noiselessly by,
Mirrors blank of me.
When at last the house stands
In order under the sun
I am not more desolate,
Though strength gather my fingers
And calm take over my head.
Remembering the dead
Will make me ready to die
And far less prone to crave
Dying for all I put up with
From all I have never done.

A life so terribly long
Was never what I had dreamed
When the joyful crown my head
Wore was outphantomed by one
Fleecing the hidden core
Under my navel. Each person
Could tell from the weight of the softness
I carried upon my breast
I had come to a quickening time.
The quickness is not lost
When the best of it slows in me.
Time is not up to the folding
Of so much in a single day.
The leaf will fly onto the leaf
Without disturbance of blood,
The bright, carrying winds
Overwhelm in softness
All that are dressed to face
Lamentable lives.

My life is a probe
For nothing else.
It waggles and can whirl
And whirl like a magnetized
Compass and still
Return to true
North, and the wonder
Of this will not diminish.

If I am to be
Wrapped in this peace till my death
As a small trenchant thing,
I will not complain, but if
The whirl at the back of my head's
Soft crown spreads to stir up
What I have known, however
Remote from my sphere of the now,
I will never do any more
Than rest and pretend not to rest.

To weep is a privilege
I am thrust into rarely,
When the preciousness of tears
Dissolves my unworthiness,
If I say I am ready to die,
And am ready, even so.

The Good Politician at
His Constituents' Party for Him

Your enlargement of me has made me the Less-than-Myself
I have chosen to blur in by operating through you
For all of us.
       This is what you cannot applaud,
Thoughtless hands; and in deadly equality
Likewise not turn the other way on me.

You have narrowed it down for me, even when the brawling
Organs of my flesh are drunk on our unanimity
And lights around a giant hall, lights small and large, pop
Themselves on and on in an air similar to drink.
The child
I once was, has never been
So strong. I am nothing
Or a cripple;
Who has thrust behind him by main force into some darkness
The struggles not to resent the inequities
Justice deals out,—intolerable mystery!—
And who shows the vestiges but as a plain
Deadening excess of cheer.

Inevitable Apocalypse

Lidding my stunned eyes in a deepening bed,
I give up a complacent dream. The dream
Of brute complacency cries out for blood.
The bloodless revolutions are a dream.
The Hill of Skulls, the Rainbow and the Flood

Will never go. On the fountains of the waters
The Star called Wormwood is about to dawn.
Down, down my spirit goes before the slaughters
I did not help to stop, I who should have grown
An open heart taking in all that matters.

The margins of the heavy Book are dark
With annotations, and the dream I read
Peers through slit-windows of a riding ark.
I sift my slackness in the winnowing need
That arms the world and makes its hungers stark

And let a lightning triumph scythe the Jews.
I see by the black light of that Yellow Star
The world-blight bombs. Dreamlike, the triumvirs
Of strategy sustain hysterical calm
While blood runs dry in a dream of machines,

Their triumph. Their shibboleths stand supreme
Over life and death, in whose book I but sleep
To bleed my life away. Life is a dream
Canted like an ark out onto the lolling deep.
And blood redeems the time that shed the blood,
The dreaming blood.

Winning Through

Peaches in my romantic orchard sustain their bruises. I abandon them
After a fashion, having known other
Places and times as bearing the thought-box
Of less than anguish into the more than tolerance
You and I strive to bring alive.
The defeated soldiers
                    who shit in fear
And are outraged, it was no good, the dimly understood
Cause frayed like false goods,
Can still redeem themselves. The more so ourselves
Lie open
          a road
A bitter factory a library a canopied
Bed
Of our flickering fire for one another:
Not lost if ill-considered,
Not spoiled if tampered with, if somehow
Bungled. Bunglers, too, can win through. Anybody can
Who lets himself in the face of the true terror
Of not: the constant terror.
And they do. Hallelujah! All around us
They do, and don't, and do,
Beside which, love, the cancers
Spread on a sinking body.
Never mind, for all the violations
It can rise, if one, rise
As well as fall.

Stone Courtyard, Stone Monument

A Special on Communist China in the bored
Intervals I flick on the set:
The camera quails through stone
Courtyards of milling, chattering Chinese
And comes to its and my halt, snared
On the snide voice of the white-haired Shanghai
American doctor dominating a courtyard explaining
In our obsolete catchphrases how
The life's a paradise, and gains
His life by healing (not where he believes).
The quotient sickens as the patient heals
                          I am aware
                                Delicacy
And force are on the line
Here there everywhere,
In myself, I flick it off, it does not matter,
Dust unto dust,
Beliefs quail, men turn to stone,
Dust settles on the stone
Of the incurable
My ideal I am back
To my partial petrifactions, perhaps, the war
Against my boredom has to turn to joy
And stop being a war to rise at all
Not be memorialized at all
As it were in stone.

In the Genoese cemetery
Of the last age, the wealthy expended their resources
On the family group rendered in stone
Around the deathbed, to the last mole and fringe, stone,
Flared skirts and frock coats sculpted in stone, dust
On the stone.

Voicing

The human voice without fanfare conveys its affection
As though there existed organs of repose
Inhabiting cathedrals
Of sheer air inhaled

Or electricity were fitful but never lacking
For a chain of lights on an outward swing
Over the grounds
Of an open carnival.

If a man indulges his capacity
For being a more-than-fair-weather friend to man,
The favor of
His gladnesses

Will wash the throat like ale, and otherwise
Hungers are rammed down the gaping mouths
Of poor stragglers
In a stubborn body.

Someone calls out and there is an answer.
The wines of earth are stoppered for a day
And no one
Takes it amiss

Though horrors for the hunted and haunted
Do not diminish where a Spanish moss
Hangs in decrepit
Moonlight

Or the parched plain disperses moonless throngs
In the hard knots of its order of legacies
For living around
A sparse center.

Full of new thoughts in danger of turning sour,
I am not convinced by illustrations when
New fears feed
The older ones,

And more excitement peels off in the distortions
Of those who take it amiss when stalemated,
Punishing themselves
To let it be known.

A compact mummery wallops its devotees,
And the man who voices joy in the surrounding
Signs coming pure
Once in a yellow moon,

Stands in danger of being tranfixed
By his own piercings, making the least
Of thrift and bartering
Body and blood

That in a test-tube would purple. The labor-
Saving responses might bewitch a nun.
The gates throb. There
Is no other life.

The Accessible Forest

"Dear God, in the journey of this life, why
Does your viaticum . . . " The hand stood
On the page, freckled in light from nearby
Trees of the forest, and incapable.
And the man stood up beside his window, visible
To passersby, like each lost in himself.

She was finding a way among shades and shades of flowers
Beside him. He had still not designed to help her, bronzed
In his own boredom. They stuck their bare feet
On old leaves discomposing, horror
Of decomposition (he was oblivious).
Here, flush to a tree, jutted cement piers that had supported
A bankrupt amusement park swinging
Chains of lights.

Spring water rang on a stone
the being of ringing.
Her ring
On her finger shone.   She said
"If I were better dead, I wouldn't be here.
So take . . . what?
Cheer.
Plain old unvarnished cheer.
Forget it all, if you are capable,
The desk behind your window.
The grain-sown
Lines under your eyes tell no lies, the lines
On your brow are beyond my depth.
Even if I were back on my back in a tumbling
Shadow, imagining spark-showers. . . .
The gamut is under our hands, let it run
Off the bounds of the known world

Which is to know."
And
"Face of Christ on your wall
Sweat-image sorrowing
Be thankful you do not
Sweat, gagged and bound
Upon the blinding air."
He
"Now we are given a tempo to soft-pedal.
Our woods are temples of their own.
Your foot beside mine is thrown
Sufficing air, fair
In its time.

        "See, the clear pool around
        And over the broad rock
        Is foaming, foaming
        And forming a swarming foam."
"And the tree roots, incomparably alien
To your murderous tension (it will not
Murder me), my murderous
Relaxedness (Save me from myself)
Mingle unmangled. I for one am ready to turn
Around and with unwilling steps 'and slow'
Circle back around
To the room, where lost in yourself
Like everyone, you radiated a need
That made me more than a passerby, one
Who angled for just this invitation
Out. For now, that is everything."

The Urgency of Excess

Magnolias have strewn
The ground before I see
Their petals fully blown.
Blooming clarity
Inhabits but a mind
That can no longer see.
The laws that free me bind
Ungrounded urgency.

If this explosive spring
Bring to mind others, I
Will drowse back as I sing,
Sorrow as I joy.
If at a surge of midnight
I strode in joy on and on,
I did not still my heart,
It was through a war-driven town.

Say I ingeniously,
Desperately create
The flaming walls of Troy.
Pyrrhus is at the gate.
As though in the one fire,
Priam and Pyrrhus fall.
Helen too is there,
Brightness ravishing all.

Call it a wilting spring
And I am satisfied
No more, and no less wrung,
And find the selfsame pride.
Wounds will reopen and
The resurrection come.

The heart in the grand
Scale, stands dumb.

Gauds of impotent
Saturnalias
Have crinkled and have blent
Their powers around my ears.
Christmas trees burning
On January snow
Have spent their darkness early,
Purely out of show.

I am what I have seen.
Excess is here to stay.
The fray neither dies down
Nor dwindles either way.
Sorrow and joy
Expand as I expand,
Brute perplexity,
Sureness on either hand.

Thanksgiving

Planes stretched and cars pushed to converge
Us around the brilliance of linen and rough
Music of voices
Rising to nothing other than this
Invigorating autumn.
Changing leaves
Are changed.
In solid afternoon
Behold! we do homage to a daylight
Custom outlasting
The single lives.

      Not to be lost
In my native element,
Not to have gone under
Among these dominances
On my common ground,
Gladdens,
Not to have known the terrible
Pull of reversing change,
To be thrust all right
Must be taken as I am feasting, thrown
Into this bright-eyed realm
In variances of childhood beyond
Making sense.

      Children in the mass
Are bound to disappoint
The children out of that state who here thrive
On the disappointment,
Thicken as the meal progresses.
Tear-filling eyes.

Oyster morsels stuffed into spicy crumbs
Ooze from the brown glaze
Of the steaming bird.
Brown biscuits and cheese-stuffed celery,
Raisinous pies
Around roses.

Out the window under white clouds
The rose bushes are bare. These
Swimming in water, peel the blood-
Red of their petals. Across them the gay
Grandmother looks
Squarely and dimly
Through glasses she shines
In abundant idleness.
Florabundant sight.
Widowhood weaned
To another fullness. Her gray
Son retains the hawk-stare
Of a youth once startling
To all, and now to him at last.

Leaves shade to brown in one depth and then
Another in the steadily
Sinking sun out the window. In the mountain the waterfall
Is dry.
                    The prayer spoken for all
The lost and agonized is lost.
The agony
Has no bottom, before it the shame
Of any one man is bottomless,
Unfathomable,
Unassimilable in the mass.
We play ahead into

Other fractures, luxurious,
Ingrained.
Second nature burnishes the first.

Fibre I am thickening,
Hard, plain,
Open single in the double sun.

At the mercy of the resolutions
He celebrates, Narcissus presides
Over the dining table, his vision
At the mercy of his hearing,
Coming back for more.
Where expectation married
Resolution and pronounces the going good,
The groaning board
Is there to reconcile
Wilderness of failings.

The eye pumps it all back.
To live forward, thrown
Singlemindedly
Where we may be conveyed!
Fossilized shale
Crumbles from the embankment
Of the highway I will diverge
Onto from this place.
And you who will fly away, sealed from the weather, propelled
Out of ordinary time, will carry
This fatigue of exhilaration
On into night
Advancing, night not
Unabounding of still more
Strange transparencies.

He has read his way to the deaths

He has read his way to the deaths
at the back of the paper, time
for sleep has not yet come, and he
strolls under shedding trees, a length
of pavement, soon out of breath. Greyness
spirits off memories of strength.
Depression moves in: he inflects
cold comfort under cloud-parted
skies of carrion-breeding stars.

In His Age

Spangled in his age, a Persephone
Blind to his own burial, his
               sunny transformation, he long ago
Modulated
To the white hair wafting away
His stern face twenty years
Have drawn out of his mirror into the chair
Facing his.
           And the meadow still leads to the sea.

Sharks rake the open water,
The nature of things
Shows its hand,
Age inverts youth, youth
Invents age.

Petrifaction or putrefaction.

Sunglasses or a pale wash
To the depth of
Such elements of grace as melt the eye
Forever

And when the cry comes, a cry brandished
Against power power power
Unhidden, out of mind,

Nobody knows what to do with
Banked shining

The cry not enough of a cry
Is the last cry,
Hunger hunger out of mind.

What you have loved comes floating
Back in the waters, a temporarily
Brandished, health-bringing sea.

The man alone

The man alone
Reminds himself
        As shot by the arrowhead
Of intent
        As marking the pillar of a handhewn church
        As outfitting a ship
            Love eats the distance up
            That blows a sun at time
            And time will have its own
            At the expense of love.
    Is reminded of what is built into the sun's
    Visibility
        As a single mast
    For governance out for a single caulked hull
    As doctrines expounded from a pulpit
    Arrowhead fitted to the shaft
The antiquarian reminds himself
    Lover of the new born,
    The distance you are part of falls apart
    Before it wells within
        As white hulls
    Bobbing
To colonize himself is what a man can do
    Sheathe the arrowhead open the church
    Launch the ship
        Alone or not alone.

In Autumn, One Dies Over the River
For Tom McFarland

Thunderstruck by thunderstruck
Lamentations, how can I
Unleash from the heart's crystal ramparts
Praises?
        How can I not?
                Leaves have fallen and will
Fall from the crystal ramparts
Of autumn,
Rivers
Run every which way.
On the far hill her house's bleary eye
Eyes me, ready for the big drops
Of a greening thunderstorm,
Not sweet-water tears but wild
Ablution among parti-colored leaves,
Fête champêtre,
These chords, these clouds,
A burst of mere song, unashamed song.

Shamed in my integrity, I am sick
Of the suicidal arches,
             Rightly, glad
In the glorious discovery: not
To possess the deadening power
Of hardening the heart!
Let hostilities mire hostility.
If I hated, I need not hate,
Let me in turn be
Born, reborn on the side of her far
Hill that I remember,
Feigning sleep,
Glare and dazzle of the Indies in the leaves.

Death blossoming
In her old entrails humbles me, mumbler
Of humbling truths.

                    The last ivy
Trails the insouciant wall.
The integrals
Of this life perpetually bother me,
Humdrum, drummed
Up for considerations, satisfactions
Known from birth, to be known.
The horrible confessions shed their horror
As a tree leaves.
Plunder experience as the thunderstormed bee
The flower?
What can the plunderer
Do with plunder but have been a plunderer?
My entrails knot
                to have shouted
                        bewildered hatred
At those I love
                The venom of our life
Is the pace that kills. Ah, researchers
Of internal medicine, you have not found otherwise.
You I love, my salvation, crystal
Ramparts of the heart
I am born
To bear and be borne in the thunderstormed
Green fields and blue sky, dark grained
Beyond my capacity, stretched or slackened
To the four winds of my
Experience's wizardries,

Puffed
Mouths of the Winds blasting at curled
Corners of Renaissance maps; globes; spaces
Of giddiness to master and annul.

The Heady Valley

In the heady valley of persistent dreams
Given or not given to be my own
A heady virtue practised to the bone
Is crying for the gathering
Force (adaptable and yet invincible)
Of love.

        If I were to say of my drooping head
It drooped like a flower, one I loved
Might counter with saying
"Twenty years is no small contribution
I have made to the force of love.
We are ravaged, we may die or live on
And not change the conditions, that is not what matters,
That the valley be drained
Of the blooming we express by the name of flowers."
It is in the head, the mind
Gathering its strands, a little stiffly.
And if the valley of yesteryear
Haunt a public face a gardened face
Gardened valley or dream,
Never may we transgress the law of kind.

Rogue and Peasant Slave

The peasant's
Sublime face hardens in benign
Refusal to become aware of fate's
"Constrictions unto death."
Because death roughens his soil, has his countenance
Roughened.

        The smoothness of mine, I know,
Might betray me, unless
My words can exceed death
In this century of explosions,
Exploding brain
Lesions and contusions,
Of a killing pace.

I lose touch
And scholasticize what cannot be cauterized
Or exalted.

        You lose touch,
My friend, and only swing open
Your back screen door an instant on the loud
Peace of chirring in the fall haze.
The harvest moon is hidden.
Inside I respond to a mission
Of forgetting contradictions, inheriting
The old legal acts,
Hedging illegalities
As though you were doomed to be
Grizzled, unblooming, "wise."

Between happenstances
Of great decisions, little felicities.
And how could they ever really

Have been given up, the black sails groaning,
Groined, struck cheek,
And the odorless day of his necessity,
A carpet beneath his soles, the blown
Green of a sought hill, ill-concealed,
Rememberer,
Acter, actor, and the great scythe mows the heads
Of the brown grain ripened into actuality.
Gloaming.

And will you persist in bothering
With your hesitations, which are his once-removed,
Self-styled Prometheus?
Vultures of my own making gnash beaks
Over this caucus of a Caucasus.

The Widow's Future

It slides and flows
Sloppily right
Through these eyes,
The grey of night,

Until it turns
Fathomless black.
My light is on.
I can't turn back.

Looking ahead
Means look to you
And leave the blood,
Before I'm through,

At my mercy.
I need one more
Pair of drained eyes
That can confer

Clearer redress
And faultless pride.
Age's weakness
Is on our side.

Willed messages
Lump their going
Concerns with less
Than simpler ones.

I am done if
My cry's not heard.
My clock has clicked.
The cheeping bird

Flutters and bangs
His cage. Pomade
And rinse are capped.
My ink will aid

All by itself
My age. Do write.
I need contact
All day and night

With someone who
Retains his sense.
Where envy thrives,
Magnificence

Cannot expand.
I know your ways.
A widow's will
Moves by degrees

More powerful
Than I would show
Any other,
And let you know

The brunt of looks
Encountered bare.
Mine was and is
A lethal stare

Frightening me
But preparing
A vast space where
My bird will sing,

My car will dirve,
Live impulses
Not pull straight out.
Pangs without cess

Pierce and corrode
My vitals through
If soul were flesh
And you not you.

Keep your distance.
Don't go away.
My space could change
Now, any day.

Rough and tumble
Stresses of nerves
May in the long
Run build reserves.

Proud and helpless
On this stretched ground,
I may come round
Humble and strong.

Not Given

1.

Not given to this burning I am not
open to the other (burning)
not craven
          mined on a battlefield
dreaming, burned in the dreaming

2.

out of this
stream I am nothing
watercress, current-stirred pebble, minnow
of mine,
saline solution
stronger as nearer the city
built beside the stream
on principle
laughing waters

3.

salt remaining
after tears a grain
at the edge of the eye
reminder
where I have not been going
otherwise than through
floods of tears my own or others'
I have not the heart

4.

sponges, melons and sun-worshipping body
gyroscopes, decks
hooting liners
florid jowls
and the apathetic-through-hunger
and white, so to speak, bodies, fading away

5.

If in mountain darkness I am me
what could it be to be.
mounting derision
levels us all, here we are.
If we do not bother to bend for the little there is
in a long time going
do us the one favor flawing the joy
scrap in the jaws
of a glinting wrecker   and would have said bereft
                                      up to and beyond that point

6.

loneliness
has crumbled its last ash
on the well
            we are brimful
of consideration
mothered where the under-mothers live
and hear no call, and feel no fire.

Letter to Another

You ask me, from your shelter, for decisions
You daydreamed away. You never hid it from me,
Persephone of mascara and strategic
Depressions, of toils as small, deadly, and character-
Changing as the fabled pomegranate seeds,
Getting back your own.
So I defer. This page is it.

Deferment, you say?
Of air you say? Of a strong sea? Of strong
Decisiveness? I am your man.
It does not becloud expectancy
As your grey eyes wanted the hieratic
Music we heard together to do.
It does not domesticate drudgery.
Outdoors, through leaves,
Clouds, fragrance, hums,
Yearnings, the tail lights of airplanes
Fizzle out. And what did you expect?
Deferred pleasures?
                        The even temperature of a cave?
Remember hooves of Altamira thundering
In the dreams of the book whose pages we turned,
And are there, lost.
It could not be the same next year.
The macadam darkens, madam.
I darken.
You won't listen anyway.
This is enough of a good time.
A good thing, a good girl,
A good man
In all our differences
                        marked like unfair cards

As it were by your diamond thumbnail,
If you will allow me to be grotesque.

Try and stop me.
The contagion fences me in, fleeces me, it's chicken wire,
Passchendaele, Bastogne,
Thermopylae, if I can bear to keep
The frivolous note going when so many have died.
It's not my natural element.
I'm quickly disproving that.
I'll confer with the elms.
And don't call. I'm under-telephoned.

It is Bound to Be

The heaven of the resigned
Does not beckon, barbecues and minor caresses,
Fireworks on holidays and every day a holiday fulfilling
Wishes of children, horses free to roam
Imaginary pastures, bullheads pulled in
On dream hooks.
                          In gloamings,
Old men whose tobacco-stained moustaches
Mouth slow pronunciamentos.
                                      The purgatory
Of the resigned has not moved too far away.
The chaff-laden files and machines
Running down as superior ones are built
For owners less and less eager, pile up.
Funeral pyres and ceremonial lacerations
Draw attentions, major caresses
Make their demands.
                              There are more heavens
Than campfires in a cooling desert
                                      where automobiles
    Carry thicker and extra tires, whose creatures
Live by tunneling out of the elsewhere-vivifying
But here deathly sun.
The living dead
Are ceremonially invoked by those who have never been so strong

On ceremonials and all the breviaries.
Farewells hang like grapes on the vines
Of an abstemious country.
Sleepy musicians charm a restless sleep.
Unceremonious headaches
Revive compressions.
The scraggly shepherds drowse

In lost hills
        In darkening offices
Decisive men grow stronger on tentatives.
Illuminated numbers on public clocks
Run the other way round, hands the same way.
Hands force the stomach, heart hands,
Glands are too strong to be left alone
To vegetate like vines
In a country standing on no ceremony
But those of arbitrary inventions, and at that
Bewildering, passing around an invisible
Hair of the dog that bit everyone.

Surrounding Green

This surrounding green
Truth of my perception
                        heady as new
Blossom: cherry, other:
On ground or air
Is as hilarity that does not mind
Being unable to issue into
Laughter because the toss of leaves
In light, light on the lake, is all its smile,

Is as an early comer of so great
Fulfillment he would not mind early death
Nor would such destroy the smile
He is, I am,
It is so, it is my humor
That Eden was green so, day
Of Resurrection.
                    Laughing could not sting because
Dying would not, and little by little
Green, I do not mind not understanding,
Not being
Poem, this world, which is suddenly
And 'early', everyone's.

Not that I am up to this green
Sparkling and bearing light.
It is here on my verge
Foiling the vapid relapse of the longing
For fuller worlds when this is full enough.
If early and open I had known this green
Green, I could not remember
And could not get enough.

                              Early it is
Lettuce-crisp: like an edge
Of birdsong in me flowered into a million
Flat light-rinsed leaves like this
Gardening of
Sight and gladness.
                    It is no surprise
I am, green
The garden, Sun. The garden
Impoverishes its gnats singing
And stinging: a red-
Winged blackbird on the wing
Eats them.
                And an idea of black withering
Hovers below possibility,
This pure world, in its very
Animal pitilessness
Breathed and merged, given
                         undimmed for all
Perception
          I am the feel of
Ruddier than motley, lost and found, all of us,
                              The soundless clowns.

Let it be
What the miniscule flickers
Tell us in their 'destructions,'
Of perceptions, a lake taking the light
Let a mind taking
                 all this gratefully
Hummed into gratitude
                    Not knowing and caring

This regal early time
Merged
          airing
                air.

The grave
Problems suspend in air, as a leaf, one of these
Thousands, at night, awaits the chlorophyll-
Granting star to be near
Enough in its million miles
To be all of natural illumination

And if it dies bit by bit, with or without us,
It has poorly died.

The Family Reunion is filling the State Park's

The Family Reunion is filling the State Park's
Old trees and wooden tables painted green
Right out to the ledge over the waterfall.

Young men and old play baseball.

The women in flowered dresses
And those in dark shorts and halter
Sit around gossipping

Moving in their midst is the veteran
Not incensed
But driven into himself
After wasteful years
                The deaths
Of so many have displaced
His space
                      nor can he bear
The silent communion of others
Likewise drained
drained and past dreaming
to be reconciled.

See where the factory, shorted

See where the factory, shorted
Down a scant while ago
Has been rebuilt.
Windows on a larger scale
Comfort the employees.
The time coumpounds.

The son of the manager
Is mad for swimming, and the widow sews
Around the clock.
Our loves are a mockery
If their emitting waves are not kept
New as can be.

The doings of your yesterdays
Flutter beyond your power.
He executes the wills of utter strangers
As best he can, and why should it not
Quiet him down? It does not.
The chlorined pool

Sloshes its new waves in the same
Sun for one and all. He has let
The water get too warm. The striped
Chairs are too hot. And who cares?
The comings and goings
Escape your vigilance.

In the beaten light
The garden, come back to its old fruitions
Of stalk and broadening leaves,
Is on its own.
Where will you be when
The old friends declare:

"Here are the inundations!"?
The tension is high, that is another sphere.
The largesse of its roundings will not wait.
The blast furnaces go on about
The murderous business you cannot extricate
Your yearnings from.

They are your future too.
Saint John of the Cross could have gathered himself
The imprisoned years, the dusty roads
Are paved. Poor sandals such as his were
Lose their grip.
Leave for the sake of leaving, and what

Can the flashing Distance do?
Your past is what your future has discerned.
Gloom, melancholy gloom
Loses its aggravation, and mere glee
Beguiles a mere instant. You ache
For the homages to what you might have been

And have to be
In the backwash
Of this engulfing calm. The way-stations
Drum up their own trade.
It all flows this way
Through solid space.

The Old Adam

Over my head, I never feel a wave.
The well I'd drown in cleanses dwindling eyes.
When the lost forests of my morning mirror give
Scant hint of sapphire joys, the frosty sighs
Rise in the dripping boughs. Joys I conceive

Reddening in the quickness of a dream
Double and dowse the marriages they spring.
The wood and the desert dwindle while they bloom.
Night falls as quickly as a raven's wing
On milk-bleeding cactus and loam-draining elm.

Darkness is unleashed before a given
Day hauls in blood-dipped banners it has flown
Over the unnamed traffic's mobbed and even
Flow to and through the portals of the known.
The double pull of fears hungers in vain.

And when one fear dies out, another fear
Has sown the dragon's teeth. Far by a coast
Of rock and pine shivers a pallid girl
With wing-thin shoulder blades, unblest
Under a sky more plangent than a pearl.

The broadening body abandons what it wooed.
Bloody it was, new-born; and upside down.
Lute strings of sunshine tremble in the blood.
A well of black oil from subterranean
Strata struck, forces a dazzle of light.

Butterflies unleash on a thunderous beach.
Landscape mists a ridgy bridge away
Of hollow green, the Mandarin's deft reach

Of taking what he was born for, being gay.
Tirades of being calm, each losing each.

And the old Adam skimps the other Eden
Of blurring loves and doubled images.
The fugal will, playing out, is deadening
Legends of gold and myrrh and frankincense.
Purple Lenten shrouds are suddenly unveiled.

IV

Progressive Secret

I am let in on the secret of my own life.
If I had been permitted to stand on a single pinnacle
I had attained, the secret
Would be closed to me like the kernel inside a crinkled
Shell that a clenched fist cannot crack.
Like an undulating creature too far below water level
For his motions to be registered, let alone seen.
Like a party behind a sound-proof wall.
The pinnacle melts, hooray! And I am in
The party, at once host and guest,
Wearing the clothes of everyday.

Recessive

Abandoning his clarity, clarioning
His abandonment, he has seen
the time
roll back its penetralia
open to him, open
as much as he can take it in: a sea.

"I know I am a child no longer."

An open air bath, and there is
a vision through trees, sponges
his blanched
chest, the terraqueous pool
tiled and aquamarine
open to the play of leaf-shadow
over his wet lashes, he sinks
bathing in that water, himself
afloat.

And the limpness
staggers his reckoning.
He left the unloving nozzle end
in the hand of a
disappointed gardener, himself.
                              The roses, rambling all over
his trellis did not do the job.
The fulfillment
did not come up to snuff.

The wonder of a hurt
from a loving voice
blunted
a shrunken choice
in his ear.

Stretched muscles and spent mind,
he left his spent companions as they are, coming
to no harm, overpowering
image of being safe.

Every night
unchain the latch
the bullseye peephole
lungs milked of air.

His reservation is his desolation,
shame his glory, name
calmed him, and
The Great
Peace descends, white
in its instances, he cannot
rise to meet it, think
a bitter streak,
it comes to less,
he could apparently dissolve
in his bliss,
he has to blink
to stand uncertainty
within the bounds of
pacific images,
and furies are no lie.

He has enjoyed a Bokhara rug,
the white-hooped gooseberry,
three stars in a green sky,
a pair of sympathetic eyes.

"Into and out of openings
of long loves

and living hives,
I am given to my own springing."

And the simple summers.
Crystal waterbubbles flake
from the twig of willow
supple in water
and slime. The frog
dunks under the lilypad. Swathes
follow the light ripples.

Reef to reef,
roof to roof.

The child within grows
amazed at the blearing of
his fleshly windows.
It comes back to the divination of suffering
for who can stand to square it.
The branch-swart bloodings fail.
It goes on everywhere
behind the wheel
in an ecstatic bed,
coming out the other end of a problem,
the environment changes,
pleasure is good though the instruments
be blunt:
Luna Park, Luna Park, Luna Park,
red rollercoaster
plastic facings
steel struts
child's play.
He works it out.

The Ways of Imperfection

The strong man speaks to the hesitant girl
In my dream.
He goes no farther, she is no longer listening.
Here I am in my pretenses,
Breathing my share, bearing less
Than I sense I could
Know I can

One of you never gets there,
Another caroms through,
And sees it not,
Proud of his ambassadorial shame.

Consciousness my rheostat,
Politics a burning ghat
Display

Of fixations.
             And with it all the annunciation
Of a plain day.

The mushroom
Soaks up vapidly,
Flubs under the finger.
Moisture, and a stringy whitish web
Mats under the needles of the Ponderosa pine.
Star-moss.
A fidgety croaker hops in speckled shade.

In blissful space,
In hopeful time.

Who can subsist on perception taken pure,
Or do without?

In the sudden light you switch on
The electrified roaches leave your bathtub gleaming.
Another year and the movie theatre
Stows its plush ropes away.

And give your excesses:
A canvas
A fund
A night club
A dominant partner and several
Submissive ones.

Scrape and size
Your surfaces.

And what you are to do
Remains undone.

I stumbled on a comb bleached from the upper jaw
Of a skate, all but buried in beach sand.

The dragon of my own grip gropes
For a lesser hold
On a greater law.

The bronzing lifeguard has his winter life.
And one deprived
Soldier falters into voluntary
Prolongation of servitude.
The drumhead court martial
Has its homicidal way.

In my entanglements I rive
Bonds no other has strength for
And perhaps not I.

And "be precise,"
To be precise
Bothered you
Half out of your head.

The body I begged to behave
Did so in its own fashion.

Habit digs in for good.

Say I had seen the light
and pulled back, *die Winterreise*
heard in a summer moonlight.
                          Display of fixations.
Every confrontation
Exhausts the resources it bids fair
To reward with others.
                          Adulation secretes
Sleep
        and mockery.

Just watch me
Long my way
Into a simpler garden where all leaves
Wear the same hue, and summer,
Summer in the dripping leaf
Blown dry in an hour
In the self
Is struck.

I stride blind over
A rose-of-the-winds tiled into my floor
To a drive under blowing trees
Beside a bridge

Grown grey
Come round to where I am wanting.

                              Desire
Turns cartwheels over its own bright boundaries.

The needless relative goes into a becoming shyness.

                    The dry wife
Has bathed.

Inventing This World in Your Lifetime
In Memory of Charles Olson

Start anywhere, you will be back round again.
The end of the cycle brings a solid ease.
The willingness it takes to seize and bless
Glimmers within.

In the night of its first breaking, bleak,
What was not unleashed itself
To become what it is.
I am awake, my thumbs
Swell for purchase on things.

Positing and positioning
A luxury of sweet unrest
Unordnung und fruehes Leid
To be purged away.
And away.

The cycle coextends
Neither less than a life
Nor more (leapfrogging
Into prehistory:
The chalk mask uncovered has
Holes for eyes:
A first stratum:
An equal night.

Clearing the Air

The growth of years of silence took me in

I in a fearful rush took that embrace

There are the fires of a single day dying
Into the brilliant body of the fire

There is a white lily alone in a congeries of yellow ones
On long rubbery stems afloat in brackish water

There is a neighbor in the middle of his habit-forming flowers

Dry and then spilling over
The fluted pump
Draws up from
Pure springs,

I am blooded and dreaming I take
The bongings of these beings in my ears

Humdrumming it into my humming head

The backbiter I hear in my voice
Is to be squelched in the stillness
Of this very voice
   So it rise coming
   and going in its notes
      holly on the arch
   Christmasses of amity
   Times of slumber and waking
   Dancing this round

 Let the shadow fly over the snow mound
 And sun give the branches a run

There is a branching stream lively
Under see-through sheetings of ice

So easy to say, longing
For true converse
                        Its rarity
Retains the power to astonish with its ease
Heightening a time wherein lightning
Is harmless death the last
Breath breathed vacancy indistinguishable from hope
Love the wherewithal

The Gospels Harmonized
Great clock face
Great Stone Face

In the seething memory
New Jerusalem, this or that weary prophet
Stilted in his transparent idiom
Arbitrary
                        orders of angels
Orders of marriages
Among men shaken to the root
Fear is courage hunger
An edge of living
Fire in a clearing
All or nothing
Indiscernible module
Washes of sentiment
                        and what
Is to be comes truer and clearer
Than I had been led to believe
Believe!

Luminosities

Glass ripples a rainbow on its jagged edge
I give my luminosities free play
Know how impressions stagger in the long run
The cancerous secret is undone
One and two and turn the corner
Three and four and come up square

Nonplussing my energies I cannot see
A source of light for the light
Needed
Quests and questionings
And I the quest of blessed happenstance
My poor contrivances
Will never do
To go down an aisle
And lose
My chains
Taking my time in the given time

Beauties are the more bewildered because of what
Beauty let them in for
Being born
Dismayed
Loud silence will invade a room minor dooms
Not penetrate
If there are others
The irrelevance of the ruination of rain
Raining down delights
Under enslaving preoccupations
Darkness reigns

Expectancy

Swarms of frustration sting despoilers of honey.
No single hair is harmed
In the dream of my blinded head.
The willow tree bends of its nature
In the wind.

The night given over to love
Deals well with a dreamt frustration.
Feature and suture do float the storied body.
The poor hunger for dreams
Soon is done.

The poor man blinded by reason
Is the man given over to night
In the sum.
Steeping his consolation he blooms and ravages,
Ravages and blooms.

Bide my time
In a world given over to waiting
And I listen for poor lessons out of inundation.
A hunger for more than night
Is gathering my cry.

The bird shall become a flash
In the sun.
And the twinning desolation
Will soon come to a head
In a time rich as hope is poor, new as the dream is old.

Face-Crowd

1.

The Sport Palace fills
The Park of Culture and Rest
Fills with waste
Paper, the Concert Hall
Empties into light-activated streets
Love responds to love on an undertow,
Sublime, of sound and rest.

2.

The olive and the willow
Hold on tenaciously
To so much ground.
I feel it all going
Under. Find me!

There is no use
Pretending.
The poor friends are fending their accords'
Sorrier rending, rendering
Soul and soul.

3.

The Crowds of the Peace
March, a stunned face, a stunning face,
Placid eyes dormant eyes lashing eyes plashed eyes plum eyes,
This one brandishing the dyed-yarn God's eye, red blue yellow stretc
Over her flourishing head,

This one slackening his jaw,
This one wrapping energy in the candy-striped hug
Of a new dress.

Slow sunshine recapitulates
The gladdening faces.
This one rides the stress point of marred choices.
This one makes bold a cold release.
This one is struck in a strenuous gloom.
This one is lost
Declaring and comparing.
This one whiles away promises.
This one salvages his downtrodden luck.
This one eradicates
Mere pluck.
Well-meaning and triumphant are they all.

Visions of the Heart

The red orb of your own
Eye will suffer into changing

Say what crippled you
Before that revelation, expand
Your secret manifestation

You meant
So much

Dear
Friends there is no time
Like when we know who we are
And when is that
If not ever now

Reveal
What can be revealed, revel
In a changing
Cat's eye

And to be twice born, Danae's
Shower would cumber
The frail armatured
House of bone

Sinking variegations

Paint bright
And sticky, bright water
Flows from your hands, bright air
Your eyes

The waterfall milks the utmost sound of its force,
The tree strains to the light,
Calculations spin the dynamo.
Constrained among perfections, I am dealt
A humbling share of imperfection
Or a devastating share.
Light! Din! Breaking
Of light and din!
Light!

Answering the Call of Pleasure

And where to go, what
to do?
I have been here through thick and thin.
On this earth, mere seasonal fires
Will spread through a pile of leaves, flare up,
Choking in a smoky char.

So wide may I see
To so many others,
Why narrow down?

Here, here the dancer gets the jump
On his suppleness, and
Stamps once
And again for all.

A seemingly bedrock dejection
After half a life and more, finds
A universe of reasons to turn out and away,
Not spurning the gift of calm
Or scorning the distressed,
Hampered and hampering
In airs of other
Young years, O my lovely ones,
Toward passion
We have sustained
Turning to an open
Equanimity among
Loving people glad
And so bewildered they do not have time
Love is not open enough
The glitter and panache
Pall in the end.

I have come out the mouth of a meandering river,
Brute silences,
The varnished paddle plied my way through.

The Claude glass
Blurs.

Bless simplicity, bless
Complexity

I cross level on level of welcome sound, and reach
On reach of aspiration.

And I forever hang back
The eye of the mole opens his hole and no other.
The tooth of the rabbit has a long nerve.
The squirrel's tail floats.

I ride
On out through the black
Aperture, night, coming on full,
Plying the secrecies that blink
Into their surfaces when I imitate
Myself.

The sufferings
I have known are as nothing
To the joys, to those of others,
I can only love through
To them, it comes round to me,
Easters: open renewed eyes
On a single shining blade
Of grass.

Christmasses:
Thumb cloves into a brandy-drenched
Orange's rind.

I will not listen to a suasion
Uttered out of guile, pain's guile.

Play it out
Give it up
Hand it over.

Sunbeam liquor, answering eyes, the moistnesses survive.

And live through the shattering
Years of a great city on
Into chosen seclusion
Orchard, evening fire,
Robin redbreast,
A high bed

And art, art,
Stravinski
In Los Angeles, Ovid by the Black Sea,
A Canaletto
Dying in Poland

Crying out
In desire and desire's fall,
Glistening trees.

Space for Friends

The adopted
Space becomes our space.
He leapt to his own
Commemorations, exploited
His own cleverness
My leaning friend
Pressed to express his pain,

      Would have the whole burden of the management
      Of love, into a whole rise, done.

That there be no more Easter eggs of rose and blue,
Round loaves and skirted dancers?

      Ah, rain blows
      Into her mouth, into your mouth,
      The lights
      Blaze away.

Ecstatic space
Expands as I go to meet
Its whorl and whirl
Backward
And a little tiny girl   into
Her glassy hair and glimpses of another
The flushing cheeks
Of Renoir's brush come alive,
The many others.

Disclosures and foreclosures
Conundrums
To dissipate, deep
In the eye of its own time, wisdom
To expound.

And have come
Over a hill
Back into your life
In common
Giant city
1956
Forever dead
The Christian
Era blossoming
On and on.

That ministrations could disappear
Into the sordor of a sweaty indifference
Attack and mock-attack
Against some
Crystalline
Manifestations,
Craggy sorrow to empty
Peace, a middle-aged peace,
Capitulation snores over roars
Of others.

       Love
Plucks a guitar
In a melony night
Under a rankness
Of leaves and flowers
Hills and stars
Here and now.

This other
You are
Has come upon me

Brown hills ghosts of my brown hills
On an earth of earthly
Visitations where
We bring to light
An ethic for magical
Ministrations to others
With myself
Yes speak
Intimate voice
Handling regret-
Mingled exuberance
As it bucks its way
Away we are with it

Who could leech and leech
Hunger
For a dark green freshened by rain
Glad songs
We triumph on our own
Not so much a mirror
That the befriended stall
A look into the eyes
Of one another revives
All around.

Under Wraps

I am
wrapped in the blazing of
a reasoned blindness
while she wept, and am weeping

I turned away
into ecstasy over a mere mountain's
unveiling from under a cloud

I splurged, it was none other
than a squandering

I mastered
redundancy, it was only

Be still, be still

Stall and be gay

Rejoice and care

Know, and know

We are royal, indulged
in fringes
of gold, a ripple
of gold over our unresponding eyes
under their wraps of light

Here I am, the dream
spills its dram

The word
dies on the inner tongue, the red membrane
swells for its own
and is not seen and
loved for its own

Boxes and boxes of white tissue
surround the gift's sparkle

The irrelevant psychopomp
is locked in demonstrations
The fear that I grow
into fat upon me
swathes too much
away from steadiness
a walking incarnation
of desire

To go whistling after bread

White haired
pensioners fill the slate clapboards
under the flourishing oaks

Your part at least
is clear

Psyching It

To make my maiden-aunt
Psyche over
into a scale-wielding
goddess of Justice
or Aphrodite bright
from the spume!

Equalling my hunger,
my energies please just
one man, his sorrows
aerate the toothed wheels
and emery points of
common energy, serrated for spinning.

Draw a whole breath,
inhabit the largenesses
of what passes.

The painful
articulation is my own, a possibly failed
outlook, poor capsule,
blue seas,
marvels,
dry-dunking.

Here crazy,
now whoozy
from obnubilation
cloud on flushing cloud,
the diadem
I confer
upon my greying head
about as visible

as stroboscopic lights in daylight
far away
I did not know
to be so long.

Horizons of Silence
For Elizabeth Shaw

Shining in daedal
brushwork the archangel
is transpiercing the gory scales
of the glowering dragon at the unforgettable camera back
of your three-hundred-and-sixty-degree
eyes.

Lights on the farther shore have not gone out
for shining beyond your view, they are still twinkling.

A monitory
foghorn is blasting before your seen
world is born out of a white shining
burned through by the splendid clarity of the sun.

The dumb hope you are nursing all these years
has not gone dead because, poor thing, you would crush it
in your indifference.

The stolid woman kneeling
to flap out tortillas and her fearful
days of solemnity edging upon her knees
over a pavement to the garish altar
sustains her total prayer.

Upon the fair earth
of orchard there is falling
a ripe peach, and dearth
before its blush will fail.

Those wilfully excluded
come back with a vengeance.

The oily river sloshes
a dredge of dead
fish scales, a frayed pink garter,
and, stuck in harbor mud,
the winkless, toothed
star of an old cog wheel.

Encased in her glowing
facial cream, the tired singer
freshens herself, though she may be beyond
her period, walking crosstown to the glossy night
club doors.

The rentier assiduously
repairs the splintering wood
of hutches for the rabbits he sells
in the city for pregnancy tests.

The boy soldier, a horrendous pawn, is gaping his mouth
in pain for the mush
another has to feed him, under a bandage he is blind,
there are children dead and dying.

Those whose souls had been
tormented into self-insult
of a soul, emaciated to laths of concentration
stack their gone chests and eyes
against unholy peace.

They do not disappear because your luck
sweetens a haven from the threat
of loftier delights, of sorrows more

than can be borne, that are borne
to the death.

They storm through the light-stream
of your evasive loves.

The monk's plain chant goes on
and the scales of his singing
crying out for
the how and what
and why, are building common sense a sound.

Try out your cleverness
on all who will listen, there are more and more
purer and purer
nonsense out of a white collar
self-palping lips
celebration of celebrating
a hoarse and papery party's murkiness.

The Presbyterian minister in his deserted sacristy
trembling for the vacillations of his faith
finds it good
to be gladdened by the hundred degrees of surrounding
forsythia, a planting he may dare
publicly to condemn when he is sure.

The minnesinger from court to court
wandered through whistling cold
and when an air of scent and a bold flower
bade him, he whooped to welcome incoming spring,
love
lighted the dark
of his darkening soul.

The gloved visitor to a gay
recluse gardener
sees through her aquamarine bottles
tiny airbubbles and all.

Wonder, and wonder. Blunder, blunder.

Your mirror lake
is cold before the surrounding leaves
are gone.

There rises
from the pages you left on the grass, mildew
in a rainbow of prevailing green.

The many
encampments are blazing where their bias was.

The Imperial Eagle's wings find further air,
the shadows of those fluttering, spreading
things are holding sway
forever.

*Novus
sum, salutem
peto, Roma est.*

Never is the time
windless, and the windless aftermath
fruitless, and a fruitless consequence
faultless, never.

Foreshadow what you may
in earnest and in play
there comes no other day.

The crystalline
battlements of *civitas* belong
elsewhere as well as here.

Slow
tenderness yields.

Your simple
life comes to a head,
infinite point.

Masters
of joy and masters of magnificence
there are those who luxuriate
in a pure straining.

Brother men who live beyond our day,
the burghers of Calais
are draped
in the folds of an operatic
costume of bronze, their eloquence
in silence absolute.

The electric

The electric
Signs are in no conspiracy
Lining your river and mine they mean
NO MERCY NO PRIVACY
Mere verbiage
Live with them or without
The snouts of barges equally conspire
I on the concrete shore
Aware of their passage in my own
Passage
      At the rim
Of my eye the electric sign flashes,
Flashes me AWARE.

Sun and Suns
For Aaron Rosen

Among sun-worshippers
Flocking to the sea I am of them
If beyond

Lying alone on tossed sand:
To be swamped
By that poor excuse for being, me!

I am in my middle age in the clutches
Of this maniac who back in my life demands I give to serve
His voracity, my precious days.
He too treasures them.

Salmon leap elsewhere
An upsurge of waters, live joy-thrashers
Only that one way
If clocks are eyes.

Hear, hear!

My purposes coral me over.

It is the marine view beating out my soft
Waves of life, and on the underside of this mottled
Rock, the jelly-green anemone shrinks his tough rim
At a touch.

The hand that groped
A sea urchin's spine out of clear blue
Water, bleeds and heals.

Call, call, and an echo
Fills the very soul.
Distance swells and falls.

I am in it all.

I am that poor man
Who is blind to his brown floor, that low
Doctor ministering to him, unsure
Of what either could want
Does not stop
For hopelessness.

Groundswell of suffering, how can I be true
To you and not darken my pleasure?

Novelty, rococo Easter egg,
Gives way to the blazing simplicity of a sun.

The fires of my words are burning, not enough are burning.
If these coals are coals of fire
Will their ashes salve or tire?

Here a new Promethean heat
Throws the sun into a cheat,
Night lover in a sweat.

One Narcissus
Will do
As well as
Better than another.

The same flowers
Fill the mirror of some pool, languid
Hopers preen.

And over the sea breaking loose
Blinks the plane's taillight in a universe of stars.

Half-daft I watch
For aftereffects.

Had I got through to myself, source
Of what possible joy
I could muster, giving
As much as all, I would take
Time to come around, and more time.

Phantasmagoric
Depths of childhood, to gravity
I descend, levity is volatile, rise
Into my shudder
Of counteraffirmation,
A clear straining.

And to go
Back, to have gone away
Without returning
Never to have gone away
Forever green,
Or have returned,
All is a ripening
Equally at variance
With the other blinked
Possibilities

Alternatives
Suns and a single sun.

Take and twist it to your blighting fancy
For poor flights of rage
Against yourself
In others.
          The big combs of the palms
Over these sparkling combers, the flat
Sand does receive them
As is
Shiny crumbling.

Mingling Infidels

In idleness wrested
from hyperactivity
your life is led

Your limes are cut
to perfection in tepid tea

Squeeze
the essence out

You will not have recovered
cataclysmic innocence
indulged and disabused

The bogs, the mountainous shouts,
spontaneous hurricanes

The foam of
ejaculation
is equally lethargic

Ready
for similar explosions
unhinging
crystallizations

Strength binds

The essence acts
on me
in blessed
arbitrariness

This toughness will do,
more is superhuman and

without signification, less
all mushy

Fight fire with fire
wage and wager
danger
promise and promises
fruit and fire, the fire
gold and leaf, the gold
what to be a king
glorified

Revery
takes over from distinction

Shore snows
snow powders
iodine bottles
howitzers

The crescent shore
cradles bronze
surfers, on in with a shout
and out

Soldiers
die in the mangle
of purposelessness

Snow
crusts

And writhe
into perfection

I had wanted
you to be everything
this world would do
                    pearl-
coated inner whorl
of a shell

Nacreous, nauseous

Leave him
clean in his distances

The form is everything

The sources
dry up

If we have not stained
the loss there is hope for me

Movie of the plains
Indians
cowboys
farmers
dudes
managers in a sun
tanning faces yellowing straw
drying streams
on and on
to the mountains one way and across
water
mingling infidels,
cities the other way
we are

Space of Love

To survive the wrench a child

I am where I once was and have long
Failed to be

The wellspring goes dry

To be equal to the opening

The enclosed
Garden laughs
At enclosing sighs and a drop
Flashes from every leaf

To be minotaured

Haunting his endless
Childhood the tortured
Poet who tore out an enemy's eye
Screeches BOMB and LOVE
COURT DISASTER
AIM HIGH
GIVE NOTHING

The robust soldier
Rotten and misspent
Sheds his uniform
In the end
As a little child

The white weight
Of the body is singing

CONTAIN THE FRIGHT
EXPUNGE THE LIGHT

Nymphs weeping by a spring
Make light of everything

Cloudy coccoon and drying ambergris

A rounded pebble with the swirls ingrained

The butterfly
Flutters
The whale
Plunges

A trumpeting of lilies brings me round

Threshing the least of these lives
I surface thrashing
For life

Invisible fish calm their way

Flesh and blood have not withstood
Interpenetrations
Under the drug of forced
Illuminations he sees it is his wife
He really loves his
Rattan chair deepens by the sea

The dumped mistress spends all morning
Eating an egg mooning out her smudged window
The mess of her lost marriage

Her child cries out for tending
Her streaming hair runs wild
In the eyes of a new lover
To whom her eyes are mild

She who had given so much for love
Leaves it and does not seek it any more
Dying in Rome
Without the fanfare of the parched philosopher
Coddled by nuns

I for a love known
To the one beloved
Enter the eye
Of the storm
Of bliss
To bless

Ah and to lose
Even temper
Regained
In a harder loss
Restored to an all-embracing
Sense of where I am
The ever-far

Mother-wit scales down

Preservation peters out in time

Who banks those fires
Takes heart

Not for nothing I rock
By the yellow heart of the fire
It is all opening out

A Japanese flower in a full glass
Is the buffered light-buffeted sea

Power lines phase in
A million lozenges of light

Countermanding
COUNTERMAND

And the hungering
Lose illumination
It is out of my power
To bestow

The young altruist is off
Toughening his mercy
Serving the destitute

Bestirred
In a whirl I suffer
Less and less being
Freely translated
Into the world

Correspondences

The letters have not found their boxes
The flag is up the wave
Transparent
I will ask the many questions
New man
In an epistolary vein will I imagine
The round postmark fascinates
The white sheet unfolds
Disappointment could ripen in my eyes
If the box had been empty
These tricks are binding like
Stigma-unleashing pronunciamentos
Reversing the process
                        before my answer has a chance
The far side of a wave-broken sleep.

Flying Visit
For Richard Eberhart

You asked me once, and again,
And I have come fleetingly
To your locks and open houses, and your hills,
To your beleaguered schools.

You listened, I am vague.

One more effort possibly
Down the drain.

I am when I will have been
What I was to be.

Borrowing and lending I have been beholden
More than one time.

The old benefactor with a ruddy
Face from open air
Sailing where I ferried through the same slow
Currents and dark green shores
Surprisingly greeted me.

I would
Have been open, the memory
Will not come true.

I was edging into
These transformations.

I am riding all day past peaks
I flew in over.

The pillow
Of the mountain, scarped

And sculpted in snow
Floats on the far
Field of my
Travelling sky.

There was greeting I strained
To greet in return.
In returning
One, trapped in his maleness,
Brought a pregnant third wife up and in her presence
Sent regards across the continent to a hard-bitten,
Tender old girl friend my own doleful friend could stand
For just a month.
He too may remarry.

One age succeeds
Another in my eye.

The too-hesitant helping hand to me
Now is long gone by,
And my over-assertion.
We could not be bothered to reconcile.

My poor friend who had a hard time
Splaying himself lest he be splayed
Will be back to greet me.

The giant conifers stand
Tapering to the moon.

Back
To where I came from, I am
Moving, forever on the move.

One semi-luminous

One semi-luminous
Cloud shape fades into another
A thousand times
                        and in a thousand
Valleys.
                  More and more
On my head comes through
As less and less.
                Out of the wilful silence
                                it comes
Combing what it can.
                Landfalls
Come easily
        To whatever bow.
                    The blow
Has fallen and falls
And is no more than light
                out of air
Forever falling.

Date Due
